ON TIME
WITH TIME

BY GEORGE HOPKINS

ON TIME WITH TIME

BY GEORGE HOPKINS

In Association with:

ميتاني

MITANNI ENTERPRISES PRESENTS

MITANNI

PUBLISHING

Mitanni Publishing Group
A subsidiary of Mitanni Enterprises LLC
PO Box 186, Dauphin, PA 17018, USA

Cover Design by Saleem Little

CONTENTS

PREFACE

Dear reader what you are about to embark on is a series of memoirs and essays that I put together, while in prison, and all I ask is that you come to my world with an open mind to envision what I'm saying. I did what most people are afraid to do and that's bare all honestly. In no way am I trying to bash or belittle anyone. Nor am I trying to offend anyone. While you may not agree with the things in here I ask that you at least respect it because this is how I see it. Whether it is right or wrong is a matter of opinion.

"The mind is like a parachute, if left open it can save you, but if closed you are for sure to meet your demise..."

I was incarcerated in the year of 2005 for a 30 year sentence. At that time

I thought my life was over. I walked around pretending nothing was wrong, but deep down within there was a raging tsunami waiting to explode. I managed and maintained while fighting my case, with no help from the outside world what-so-ever, watching appeal after appeal get denied and thinking to myself did I really deserve this? I tried to stay in contact with my family and so-called friends, but to no avail. I now truly understood the meaning of *'out of sight out of mind'.* No one wrote back; no one came to see me; no one sent money; no one did anything and that's when I realized it was just me...

So as my journey of confinement and loneliness began I started writing *builds* and essays about my life. What I was going through (mentally, emotionally, economically and spiritually) or how I saw things in the world. I figured the best thing to do would be to save these writings and try to incorporate them into a book form, but also forward these words of wisdom to my family. And if they wrote back then it would be a plus for me, but if they didn't it wouldn't matter because it was only a *build* anyway and if they could get something positive (or beneficial) from my writing then I accomplished my goal.

I also figured that most people in the world would like to know what goes on in prison, but wouldn't it be much more interesting to know what's going on in the mind of the people in prison; their thought progressions, digressions, likes, dislikes, pain, joys and the likes thereof? Well here's a glimpse into the mind of such an individual...

ACKNOWLDEGMENTS

First and foremost I would like to give praise to "Myself" for not giving up when it seemed like that was the only option I had; for being strong when weakness was all about me; and for having the ability to ascertain who I truly am and not being afraid to embrace life from that standpoint.

Secondly, I want to send LOVE to my family (sister's, mother, grandmother and my beautiful children) for putting up with my incarceration and hanging in there with me!

Third, I want to thank my cousin, Saleem Little and the Mitanni Publishing Group for giving me the opportunity of a life time; that being the opportunity to express myself to a broader audience.

And lastly, "THE MIND"! Big Flex…Finish your breakfast! To Ms.

Perkins, I have yet to meet you face to face, but you are the truth. To Ms. Graham, the only person who seen some light in the way I write and blessed me with the opportunity to be published in her magazine "Spotlight on Recovery", but it's also on you too! The spotlight that is…

CHAPTER ONE

Change

I wonder why *change* was such a hard thing for me to do. Why did I want to continue to indulge in the lifestyle that had gotten me 30 years in prison? If only I knew then, what I know now, I would have changed, but now….it is almost too late.

Change is to cause to be different; to become different or altered; the act, process or result of changing…

Change is inevitable and no matter how much I didn't want to, no matter how much I was stuck in my ways and no matter how comfortable I

was, it was something that was
imminent. It's either change or find
yourself in a perpetual cycle of similar
results – failure after failure, negative
karma, prison and/or an untimely,
disgraceful death.

People fear what they don't
understand, and being that change is
unknown, it is feared. Change is a road
that is seldom traveled – consciously at
least - but if I was to follow the course of
change (from a righteous standpoint)
the great works would be evident.

I sat down and thought how
nature changes on a consistent basis. It
rains, hails, snows; there is summer,
winter, spring and fall. Just imagine if it
stayed hot 24/7 365 days a year with no
rain, hail or snow. Let's say,
hypothetically speaking, that the
summer told the other seasons *"I'm not
going to let it rain, hail or snow*

anymore and I will not let the winter over take my heat". This would spell disaster for humanity and every other life form on this planet. All because the summer didn't like, or couldn't accept the winter. The oceans, seas and rivers would dry up. Plants, crops and trees would die - - - along with us!

Fortunately, this isn't the case because nature is in tune with change, but we must take these examples and apply it to our lives where ever we see fit.

Statement of Change

Whoever thought I'd be at this point…from a cold savage to *God*; and the process wasn't easy. I remember saying that I wanted every child to feel how I did and thus came the digression.

From stealing out of stores, lying to whoever was in my face, hating everyone that wasn't me (only to find out later on that I actually hated myself too), wearing a façade of false bravado and machismo, pretending I was tough (or actually feeling tough) to everyone in my face, but deep inside I cried so much that my chest would hurt. I threw rocks at cars, used foul language in my feeble attempt to be grown, got into all types of fights and eventually stopped going to school.

What Was I Thinking

I smoked weed, but not because I liked it, but instead it was my way of coping with life; my way of escaping reality. Cigarettes, Black and Milds and PCP would follow in succession a few years later. I drank beer and liquor (how could I not do any of this when my father gave it to me religiously?), I also popped pills and sold drugs.

My life began to crumble right before my eyes! If only I could see then, what I see now and view life how I view it now. My brother brought me some information that I couldn't believe. He said I was *God*. How could I be *God?* After all the stuff I did? This was the seed that needed to be planted, even though it wouldn't be watered for many years to come.

In and out of jail I went until one day I had no desire to live. A death wish; if you will. That was the beginning of my transformation. It took me not having anything or wanting anything to begin to focus on *self*; to begin to break down (to take the head of these four devils) my internal soul and create the *God* that everyone is searching for. ***Good Orderly Direction*** is

necessary in striving for perfection, but
nothing is easy – so says the Quran –

لَقَدۡ خَلَقۡنَا ٱلۡإِنسَٰنَ فِى كَبَدٍ ٤

"Verily We have created man into toil and struggle."

Chapter (90) sūrat l-balad (The City)

-Yusuf Ali:

So struggle is ordained, however, it
will eventually bring about ease. So
now, I accept all hardship with open
arms, knowing that some type of ease
will relieve my worries. So the question,
"Am I changed" need not be asked. Just
watch and my actions will speak
volumes about me. Peace!

أَفَرَءَيْتَ مَنِ ٱتَّخَذَ إِلَهَهُ هَوَىٰهُ وَأَضَلَّهُ ٱللَّهُ عَلَىٰ عِلْمٍ وَخَتَمَ عَلَىٰ سَمْعِهِۦ وَقَلْبِهِۦ

وَجَعَلَ عَلَىٰ بَصَرِهِۦ غِشَٰوَةً فَمَن يَهْدِيهِ مِنۢ بَعْدِ ٱللَّهِ أَفَلَا تَذَكَّرُونَ ﴿٢٣﴾

"Have you seen he who has taken as his god his [own/low] desire, and Allah has sent him astray due to knowledge and has set a seal upon his hearing and his heart and put over his vision a veil? So who will guide him after Allah ? Then will you not be reminded?"

Surah [45:23]

-Sahih International

As I read this repeatedly, it became more evident what my problem was, but at first glance- on the surface of

these words – my comprehension of this
was shadowy (at best). How could a low
desire (something that I wanted or
longed for) be a god over me/or to me?
I wasn't accepting that due to my
infantile understanding, and I fought
tooth and nail until one day I had to just
bear witness to the truth.

I took my low desires and moved
them to the forefront not really
understanding the cost I was about to
pay…. My life!!!

When I thought back on my
history, I saw how remised I was in all
my actions, in all my thoughts and in all
my decisions.

How could I let my poverty back
me into a corner to the point where I
could see no light no life or no power,
and the only solution for that was
money, *so that became my savior.* I

remember praying to God night-in and
night-out, and obtaining *nothing but
hard times, hunger, nakedness, and put
out of doors.* However, at a young age, I
knew that the only thing that could
solve this problem was money and the
quickest way to get it in my eyes was to
break the law and eventually become a
parole violator fugitive on the run.

So I put money before everything
that I claimed to love, but tricked myself
into believing that I was doing this for
my loved ones, to accomplish what I
never could accomplish. It was like a
dog chasing his tail (we know he's not
going to catch it, but still the dog keeps
going in circles until he gets tired). In
fact, the only thing I did accomplish was
going to jail; hurting the people that
loved me, and becoming the definition
of a deadbeat father. All of this for
money. Not knowing (or maybe not
caring) that this *idol* I allowed to

become my *God* could actually save me from nothing!!! It couldn't save me from pain, a lack of love, emptiness, loneliness and so much more! However, it did save me from physical poverty, but in doing so, it took me to the depths of moral corruption, a heartless beast and a down- right evil person which brought me to the worse poverty of all...

A SPIRITUAL POVERTY.

Before I was introduced to marijuana, cigarettes, *Black and Milds* and *wet* (PCP), I was formally known as a person with good health. I played sports, and had aspirations of someday going to college to play ball, but when I started smoking weed, the drive I had to play sports came to a halting stop. I mean I still played, but it was obvious that my mind, body, and soul were somewhere else. I was too young to be washed up, but in so many ways I was just like a drug addict who thought that he still had it. And the one thing that I desired the most (from a positive standpoint), which was playing sports and getting out the hood was suddenly stifled by this low desire to get (high). I was *chemically imbalanced...*

As my lifestyle slowly changed, I no longer went to high school to play ball, but instead, I went to school high! After a few encounters with the law, I was put on parole and when on parole, you are not allowed to smoke weed, but I couldn't stop. It was either stop smoking or go to jail, so I took my chances every- time and *anytime* I was on parole. Of course I violated plenty of times, being sent to prison because of my carelessness. Was I really that weak or was the drug just that strong? I eventually started smoking PCP because

the P.O. didn't test for this. It was a
different high, but I managed, and
steered clear from violating. However, I
was destroying my life.

When I think back on it, I was no
better than the very people I was selling
crack to. They had an addiction that
they paid for and then I took their
money and paid for my addiction. These
drugs (my low desires) became my *God*
and ruled me. And it's safe to say that I
couldn't function without them. I once
read, *"The body is the temple of God and
that Spirit of God dwelled in you."* Now
if this was true, then this means that I
was destroying the house that God lived
in, and if he lived there didn't that mean
we were one in the same? So now, I ask
how this low desire could be *god* over
the *God* in me. Of course it couldn't be,
but what it boils down to is a war
between two wolves in my body - - one
good and the other bad. Whichever one

I fed the most always won the battle. I think it's paramount to say that I only feed the *god* within now.

So now, I ask you to recollect seeing what (if any) low desires that you have, at one point in time become God over you.

Plan to Improve

I plan to improve by not only changing my outlook on how I see life, but also by implementing these things in my everyday walk. I adopted 12 principles to guide me through the *"Valley of the shadow of death"*. These principles are **"Knowledge, wisdom, understanding, freedom, justice, equality, food, clothing, shelter, love, peace and happiness."**

I had to learn that the most important person in the universe is ME! I beg that you don't look at this as being selfish. The reasons why I started thinking this way is because I learned that the first law of nature is *"self-preservation"*, meaning that I had to save self before I could save anyone else...

By continuously striving, perfection will be met in no limit of time. Change is the course that needs to be followed, but from a production output. Time reveals all things, so within that matter, all will fall into place....

Responsibility must be established or all that is done will be in vain. Responsibility is your ability to respond to pressure positively. When we accomplish this, discipline is the outcome. The word you find in discipline is disciple, and of course there were twelve. The number twelve represents, love, and that is the only way to improve, by having love for you. So if you love yourself you will go through hell to make it right. Or in this case...

IMPROVE.

I hope that whoever is reading this is in a very peaceful state (mentally and physically). All that I ask is that you follow my lead when comprehending my words. Nothing in life is easy; nothing worth having anyway! So why is it that we constantly search for the easy way out or for the easy things in life? I'm used to hearing people complain about how hard it is in their life and I've done the same up until now.

There's a saying that goes
"adversity defines true character" and if
this is the case what kind of people are
we? Better yet, what type of man am I to
succumb to the pressure of the world?
Things that come to mind are weak,
impatient, unintelligent, a follower and
so on…..

These can all be corrected once we
learn (and accept), that struggle is
ordained for all of us. What do you
mean that struggle is ordained? I'm
saying that it is inevitable; it's going to
happen whether we want it to or not. So
it's best to get prepared for the storm.
However the storm manifest (within)
first, so the inner self is the most
important to be assayed. Mastering the
internal wars takes precedence over
everything else – especially when you
understand that everything comes from
within!

Even the Holy Quran backs up
what I'm saying in its writing ch.94:5-6:
*"surely with difficulty is ease, with
difficulty is surely ease".*

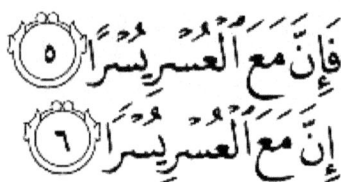

فَإِنَّ مَعَ ٱلْعُسْرِ يُسْرًا ٥

إِنَّ مَعَ ٱلْعُسْرِ يُسْرًا ٦

**For indeed, with
hardship [will be] ease.
Indeed, with hardship [will be] ease.**

[Surah 94:5-6]
Sahih International

This shows and proves that
hardship is a part of life, but it does not
go without notice for every hardship an
ease comes about.

Follow my lead for a
second......When a person works out

(physical training) a struggle takes place, difficulty and/or hardship – be it calisthenics, resistance weights, push-ups, pull ups – etc. The ease that comes after is how your body feels when you are finished – its extreme beauty – i.e. Good healthy heart rate that beats with tremendous power, which will enable oxygen to circulate throughout your body and bloodstream. You will be healthy and at the very least have a stunning body. Or just think about the planting of a seed into fertile soil. The seed which is alive (whether we recognize this or not is a different story) is in a dormant stage and has to be kick - started (if you will) from the pouring of water. The water to the seed is like a fibrillator to a man who has flat-lined. Once it seeps through the shell the seed has the hard task of pushing its fragile roots, not only through the shell itself, but through the tough, rough and rocky soil.   Which is not easy at all, but the seed never complains. Once firmly rooted in the soil, it has the job of pushing up through the earth at which time the ease comes. The Ease…..The Joy….Happiness…..in this case is synonymous to the beauty we see from the seed which has grown to become a lovely tree, plant, flower – etc.

History shows that in order for ease, happiness, beauty, etc., to come about, hardship, difficulty, pain and whatever else relates to these worlds has to happen...

All the great people before me; Jesus, Moses, Abraham, Martin Luther King, Harriet Tubman, Rosa Parks (and so many more). They all experienced grief, dismay, sadness or death, but the reward afterwards can be equated to heaven.

So who am I to expect anything less than what they went through? I think that is selfish. Complaining about a situation never makes it better. You think I'm not unscrewed immensely at the fact that LEGALLY, I'm a slave according to the 13th amendment? Or what about the fact that my support system ceases to exist, in fact I'm being treated as if I never existed!!! So, I have no money, food, or hygiene. Can you imagine being locked up for 9 years and having no one to write, call, or email? Having no pictures, getting no visits and the woman that claims she loves you is loving another man? All this hurts, but nothing more than the realization that I know my cell mates better than I know my own children! That my children (under the carless supervision of their mother), are being raised by every, and any man in their mother's life; calling that man dad and whatever else, which is something I would never allow my children to do under my guidance. Now that's pain!

This may be the deciding factor on why so many people go out and commit crimes again. Can you imagine being left for dead, by everyone that claims to be family or friend, only to survive in the end? Having people that you don't know, who more than likely hate you because of the color of your skin, treat you less than a man, talk down to you, deny your visits, set you up; lie on you, lock you in for nothing, beat on you etc. Plus not having a woman (who is the embodiment of heaven) to talk to, to touch, kiss, rub, to....................SEX, LOVE, HOLD; TO SMELL (not only the fragrance she wears, but her natural

Divine scent). When all of this is snatched from a man it leads us straight to savagery and once there many never recover. The hardest thing for us to do is get out of prison because they (the powers that be) design this so that we are always one step from failure – not to mention that they don't want to let us go anyway. The second thing is adapting to society. This is not a cake walk either, being that we have every element in the physical world working against us. But knowing what I know now, I welcome the pressure that the world has to offer – not because I enjoy hardship, but instead because of the diamond I will become once I see through it all. In addition, once I see through it, I will feel like Kanye West....*You can't tell me nothing?"*

Peace!

Fighting

Contrary to popular belief, not everyone is a fighter, and it is easy for me to say that not all people like to fight. At least I was not a fighter, so you know I did not like to fight. However, that quickly changed. Especially growing up in a neighborhood where children were encouraged to fight (physically) to survive. Therefore, they picked on children less fortunate, smaller than them, weaker than them. Not to mention the video games that displayed nothing, but killing, gun shooting, and destruction. Including the television, that portrayed the same thing. Because of these images projected into my mind's eye, I began to see fighting a little bit different – as if it was okay to do – I mean why else would they have it on every television station, in every movie, in every video game and in damn near all music? Whether it was the good guys or the bad guys, fighting or killing was the result. Once planted into my subconscious mind these images would re-surface every so often, which produced a violent act on my part. However, what goes un-noticed is the hidden hand that brings all this about!

There was a book written by Iyanla Vanzant called "*The Spirit of a Man*", in which she said on page 210,

"That universal law responds to the energy of our consciousness by creating circumstances and situations that mirror the mental and emotional energy we send forth."

After reading what she wrote, and applying it to what I have seen and been through, I now can understand why the world is the way it is and why I went through what I went through.

There have been numerous situations in the past of mass murders. Senseless acts committed by individuals whom they determine, in most cases, to have mental disorders, and in some cases, they have no answer at all. However, could the universal law that Ms. Vanzant was speaking about hold any weight to today's tragic events? I think so.

As the years came and went, I managed to become a thug, a savage, a beast with very little remorse for anyone and it seemed that I liked it. It brought excitement to my life. Let me explain: At one time, some friends and I got high off stealing cars. This was a major thing and we did it every day. We knew that we could be arrested, but we did not care. Even worse, death from behind the wheel – as we were constantly in high-speed chases. I remember one day that I was in a high-speed chase in the summer of 2000. I was riding in a Lex Truck smoking heavy weed, music blasting, and making crack sales as if the law never existed. The owner, whose wife ended up reporting it stolen, lent this particular truck to me,

I lived for the car chases, shootouts, fights and whatever else that complimented the streets. Therefore, when this occasion arose, I was up for the challenge. Driving down the block in Harrisburg, PA , I noticed two police cars following me and even though I was dirtier than Fred Sanford (carrying drugs, guns and paraphernalia), I secretly hoped that they would hit the lights. Of course, they did. I went from zero to 90 quicker than an addict could pull from his stem. I literally smoked the cops and was smooth sailing. However, I know as everyone else does that you cannot outrun the police radio, so I had to get somewhere fast. There were cops everywhere, in every direction, and while I had a good lead on them, there were coming.

At this time, I was up to 100 mph in this small city, and it was on a Sunday. This is important because as I am speeding (so high that it looked like I was driving in slow motion) there is a little girl of about 7 years in age who is crossing the street to go to church. However, she is oblivious of me, and I am now at a crossroad! Do I hit her and keep going (just to avoid prison) or do I hit the break, flip the truck, and ultimately kill myself? My mind was set – as I flashed back to "New Jersey Drive"

– smiling to myself like I am too superb a driver and skillful enough to dodge her and make the great escape I was putting together. To make a long story short, I did not hit her, but I did go to jail and this is one example of how I did bad and evil or harmful things just for the love of it.

   As I began to learn more in life, I found out that I am not the only one who knows that a thing can be bad, harmful, or evil to self and still do it! For example, doing drugs, knowing it can kill and will destroy the mind, the body, and soul. Using excessive seasonings on our food as if you will not get high blood pressure (and that is if you do not already have it). Smoking cigarettes thinking that we cannot get lung cancer; breaking the law like there is no justice system in place just for that.….However, why is this? I heard

that we are easily, led in the wrong
direction, and it is hard, to be led in the
right direction. While reading the Holy
Quran, I stumbled upon a scripture that
made it plain. In 2:216 it says

كُتِبَ عَلَيْكُمُ ٱلْقِتَالُ وَهُوَ كُرْهٌ لَّكُمْ وَعَسَىٰٓ أَن تَكْرَهُواْ شَيْئًا
وَهُوَ خَيْرٌ لَّكُمْ وَعَسَىٰٓ أَن تُحِبُّواْ شَيْئًا وَهُوَ شَرٌّ لَّكُمْ وَٱللَّهُ يَعْلَمُ
وَأَنتُمْ لَا تَعْلَمُونَ ﴿٢١٦﴾

**Fighting has been enjoined upon
you while it is hateful to you. But
perhaps you hate a thing and it is
good for you; and perhaps you
love a thing and it is bad for you.
And Allah Knows, while you know
not.**

[Surah 2:2??]
-Sahih International

This is the science of all my
problems right here!

Fighting depends upon you and the first (and most exigent) fights start within self. We must be able to overcome our own twisted and wicked machinations! If we do not, we will forever continue to indulge in things that are contrary to righteousness, civilization and the most important --- LIFE, and we will love every second of it.

Influence

One of the main things that influenced me growing up in the late 80's and early 90's was rap music. Of course, at the time, and for a long time, I was oblivious to it. As I look back on my life and the transformation that it took on, it is easy to see the connection between the two.

I rushed to the music stores every month to spend my parent's hard earned money on these rappers: N.W.A., Mobb Deep and Bone Thugs and Harmony, Jay-Z, Biggie, 2 Pac, DMX, The Lox, Redman, Snoop Dog, Ice Cube, Scarface, and a whole slew of other rappers. Rappers that I deemed to be nice, and they were at their particular craft, but none had any substance, consciousness, or positivity for the children.

Some say, "So what," or "What does this have to do with anything"? Well, for a while – since I can remember – there was a saying that "ART IMITATES LIFE," and this held true for some time up until "LIFE STARTED IMITATING ART." Yes, rap is a form of art as is all music.

What happened was rappers were imitating so-called gangstas and thugs in the streets, and that is not to say some of them were not in the streets, but they

took their admiration of these criminals
with their criminal acts and put it on
paper, then pushed it out through in
their music. Then what happened was
the younger generation that got a hold
of these tapes and c.d.'s, whose minds
were so fertile, began to take on these
roles rapped about in the music. Thus,
the role reversal was complete. Rap is
one of the strongest voices of the people,
and obviously, these musicians did not
know the power of their music, either
that or they did not care.

Follow my lead .....

Growing up, I NEVER HEARD
THE WORD "NIGGA" until I started
listening to rap music! I had no idea
such a word existed, nor did I know what
it meant. Even though we used this word
as a term of endearment, I did not know
that this word was high-jacked from an

era in history, from a group of people that used the original word (nigger) as a way to degrade black people by calling them ignorant, a dead people, stupid and less than human! "Nigga" quickly became a part of my vernacular as it did with every other child my age. I could not understand for the life of me why adults (with the slightest amount of sense) would always cringe or correct us (children) when we used that word.

Rappers made it cool to go against the law; to go against our parents; to go against righteousness. They glorified the fast life; selling and using drugs, killing people, nice cars, pretty women, prostitution, going to jail, hating the police, and doing whatever is necessary to get ahead – no matter the cost. They made it seem as if this was the only way, and it is safe to say, "That I was brainwashed." I was calling women bitches, hoes, and whores; having sexcapades: making them do things they did not want to do; treating them just like the concrete I walked on. It did not bother me one bit – not even when I thought of the fact that I had a mother, grandmother, sisters, and a daughter who were all queens in my eye.

I was convinced that selling drugs was the best way to make real money (little did I know that the average drug dealer barely makes minimum wage (sometimes less) when it is all said and done). Therefore, I sold drugs without a second thought about the children who would be hungry, who would be homeless, or without clothes due to their parent's addictions. I even had sex with some of these women, I dare say was clean and disease free in exchange for drugs.

I never shot and killed anybody, but the intentions in my heart got me convicted the same way I would have, had I actually succeeded in my attempts. This does not mean I am not a murderer. Every time I sold drugs, I took a part of someone's life; a part of someone's soul; their intelligence, morals, love, dignity. I was ultimately killing them softly. I sit down and think how many times I murdered the happiness of someone's child because of my own selfishness. I think about the way I may have helped to kill someone's relationship, someone's dreams, aspirations, or the way I essentially committed homicide on the bond my children and I would have had due to my incarceration.

Going to jail was like the rite of passage according to these rappers – if not consciously definitely unconsciously.

This is what solidified your spot (if you will) as a hard-core street dude. To come home from jail, without snitching, was the last piece of the puzzle. It let everyone know that you were real, thorough, or a person who could be trusted. In most cases, it was like a holiday when you came home: drugs, drinks, parties, guns, women, money, clothes, and cars – etc. All to bring you back into the fold of the very thing that took you out of it. Where is the intelligence in that?

Damn near every rapper smoked weed or drank alcohol. This was the "in thing" to do so of course I followed their footsteps. I wanted to be so much like these dudes, that I actually was smoking weed before I even knew how to inhale! Crazy, right? No, I did not know how to inhale, but the dudes I was smoking with saw me wasting their precious

marijuana, and they quickly taught me
the art of smoking. I became very
proficient. I tried to capture everything I
heard in the music from partying,
clubbing, tricking, not going to school,
fighting – everything (they) called real!
Boy was I taught. In fact, I probably was
influenced more (by my own people)
than what happened in the 1700's and
1800's.

    Being from the hood, (as we so
eloquently put it)made it that much
more easier to dislike/hate the police,
but to get if from your people in the
music you loved to hear added so much
more spice to it. It was like on sight with
me. Any and every time I saw the police
–whether they were kicking in a door or
saving someone's life – the same
feelings would arise that the cat and
dog, or cat and mouse had for each
other.

I am fully aware that some of the
characteristics that may have led to a
"way of life" for others and me may
come from different roots, and if this
were the case, rap music would have to
be the water that helped these roots
grow. These rappers, who say that their
not role models (or that they did not ask
to be one), have to know that children
and in some cases young adults, look to
them for many things, i.e. fashion, new
and cool language (ebonics), how to
treat women, and anyone else in their
life. They paid attention to how the
rappers made money and so much more
that you could not even imagine.
Knowing this, wouldn't it be wise to
encourage our youth – the very ones
who are to lead the future – in the way
of civilization, righteousness and
spirituality? It is our duty to encourage

our youth in anything other than evil, wickedness, and immoral acts.

Well, some rappers do rap in a positive way, but they hardly get any recognition because record companies will continuously shuffle your album to the back, until you get with the program. What I would like to say to these rappers that sell their soul for the sole purpose of popularity and money is parallel to what Jesus said to this disciples in Matt. 16:26 *"for what profited a man, if he shall gain the world, and lose his own soul"*…..

I would like to challenge these rappers to see who can make an album (not a song) that has some type of substance in it. Alternatively, are they too disinclined to give a thought doing it? You bare a heavy load when you put that microphone in your hands and I do not want my children to grow up wanting to be drug dealers, gang bangers, womanizers, or drug users because of something they heard in your music. You have an opportunity to redeem yourself by helping to save our future generations. Please do not let us down! Remember, if WORDS CAN HEAL, THEY CAN DEFINITELY KILL...

P.E.A.C.E
Proper Education Always Corrects Error

How many believe in keeping their word? What does it mean to keep your word? Well, in the Webster Dictionary "keep" is defined as being true to something; to fulfill a promise or other verbal commitment. And "word" is a promise, assurance or guarantee.

So, now I want to know how many times have we done this, gave a promise, assurance or guarantee to someone and didn't keep it? Better yet, how many times have we given a promise, an assurance or guarantee to ourselves and didn't keep it? This might not seem important, but it is! I'll show you in a minute what I'm talking about.

Whether we know it or not "Your word is very powerful", in fact, in the bible (John 1:1) says: "In the beginning was the <u>WORD!</u> That means to say that the word was here before any and everything, except thought, which comes from the mind.

Then it says the <u>Word</u> was <u>GOD</u>. That's a profound statement! It's saying that the word and god are synonymous, which is one and the same and/or equated to each other.

So to "keep your Word" means to be true to your promise, assurance and guarantee to others and yourself –which ultimately means to be true to God! To Fulfill your promise to God. The only way to do that is by doing it to each and every one of us. God is real and not a ghost. He lives through man according to the bible (check Psalms 82:6).

Can you imagine not keeping your word to God? Well, just like Jesus said to his disciples in the parable he gave in Matt. 24:45…."Inasmuch as ye did it not to one of the least of these, ye did it not for me". This was said because the least of them, which was us, and God are one and the same. So anytime you don't keep your word that's exactly what you are doing. Not keeping your word to God!

Plus, God doesn't break his word; in fact, in my studies there is a decree that asks "have you not heard that your word shall be bond regardless to whom or what"?

Answer. "Yes, my word is my bond and my bond is my life and I will give my life before my word shall fail". This tells you how exigent it is to keep your word. Look at the questions and break down the words. Have you not heard that your (word and God are interchangeable) shall be (shall means future tense; something that will happen, and be is an action (meaning bring into existence) bond (bond means togetherness to be cohesive, the act of unifying) to whom or what.

So the questions becomes: Have you not heard that God shall manifest righteous actions in your existence and

never break them (or be broken)
regardless to whom or what?

Answer. Yes! My word is my bond and
my bond is my life and I will give my
life before my word shall fail.

This is a supreme answer, but I
want to build on the last part which says:
"I will give my life before my word shall
fail". What this is saying is that your
word is more important than your life!
So every time you break your word, you
die inside! How many people believe
this? It's easy to see where slogans like
"death before dishonor" and "if your
word ain't sh*t, you ain't sh*t comes
from. So how many will give their life
before their word shall fail. I hope that
all of us will.....

This is the thing though; we have
to be careful about what word we keep.

Because as John says in 1:14 "The word
became flesh, and dwelt among us".
This is in itself shows how omnipotent
words are …. How easy it is for us to
speak things into existence…. And
always, remember, <u>words can heal and
words can kill</u>. Solomon says it like this
in Pro. 18:21 –"Death and life are in the
power of the tongue, showing and
proving the potency of your word.

Proper

Evaluation

Amplifies

Correction

Effortlessly

Incarceration.....
….Powerlessness……Confusion….

Yesterday I spoke with my son on the phone and my heart cracked into pieces! My young God told me that he didn't want to live with his grandmother (his mother's mom) anymore because she is treating him badly, and allowing her husband (who is not his blood) to beat and smack him in the face for no apparent reason, and even if there is, I'm sure that it could be handled differently. Also, that she was neglecting him. The most powerful thing he said was "she don't love me dad". Now whether this is true or not doesn't matter because this is how he feels inside, and almost everyone, especially children are going to make what they feel their reality! While this may seem like nothing to people reading this, I beg to differ. First, let me explain that I, his father who will be in prison for a long time (so everyone thinks) and has been since he was one

year old, and his mother who is free
(physically) is mentally and chemically
en-slaved to the point where she's losing
everything! Yes, even her sanity. So in
many respects, I'm in a better position
than she which is

NO POSITION AT ALL.

My young God, who is nine years
old, was actually crying, kicking and
screaming when he found out his
grandmother was at the door of his
mother's house to pick him up and take
him home. All I could do was listen as I
came to the realization that my jejune
ways and actions in the past put me in
an uncompromising position which
allowed this government to effortlessly
rive me from my children, the pain I
experienced (if not the same) is parallel
to what my ancestors went through
when being auctioned off in slavery! I

spoke to him and explained that there is a science to everything in life, and that God does what is necessary in life to accomplish his goals in the best manner. That it was important for him to get back home and listen to grandma; that he should respect every woman in his life regardless to how he feels because feelings are like illusions and can sometimes trick you into believing something that is not true. Not to mention that she's in control in my absence, and that I approved of her method of discipline for now. Needless to say, he wasn't buying it, but had other choice than to comply with these rules.

However, my main concern is WILL he continue to comply when he gets older or just rebel the same way I did? See these are all things that will cause or push children to run away from home, to join gangs, or turn to the

streets for comfort (selling drugs or
even using them) to escape their present
condition! Trust me, I know better than
you could imagine. I fear the day when
I might call home and hear something
crazy happened to one of my children,
all because I was searching for
something outside of myself.

CHAPTER TWO

Patience

To have patience is to become a patient in your walk of life and the only medical treatment is your endurance which will crystallize your understanding and character giving you the virtue that is needed to keep on pushing……..

Everything starts with patience or at least it should. Patience means to endure trouble, hardship, annoyance, or delay without complaint or anger.
Persevering.
Persistant.

I always heard that "Patience is a virtue" I continuously repeated it without knowing the true meaning of it.

Virtue means moral excellence and righteousness; goodness!

Now that I know that, shall I continue? So much of my problems, trouble, pain, hardship, annoyance and anger came from rushing into things without contemplation, without taking time to rationally put my thoughts together. The great enemy of patience is instant gratification. For whatever reason we as a people, want things when we want them instead of working for them and being patient. So many times throughout our lives, this is the reason why we fall short of our greatest potential.

There is really no reason to rush into anything because when this is done intelligence is not included. This is one of the reasons I was breaking the law instead of working. I was running myself into an early grave because I was not living correctly. This is the reason why my children are growing up in a single parent household instead of with both parents.

Patience is something that cannot be forced on you, but it has to be learned, it is almost like a necessity of life.
Follow my lead.…..

Some many times in life we accept things that we see, or hear, on face value instead of breaking down all the information; instead of doing our own investigating; instead of …… Well, you get the point. When we take this jejune (in other words unseasoned or infantile) approach we do ourselves a grave disservice, and this goes unnoticed, but only to the individual who is easily swayed.

Good things only come

I remember when I first heard this slogan "GOOD THINGS ONLY COME TO THOSE WHO WAIT". I will latch on to it the same way a baby does his mother's nipple when feeding I used this slogan so loosely – along with everybody else – not fully understanding the meaning or what I was prescribing to the people listening, but it was merely out of ignorance. One day I sat down and asked myself, "how could anything good come to anyone who just sits back and waits for it to come –with no work whatsoever? That's so close to a oxymoron I can't tell the difference. In life you have to work for everything – be it money from a job, nice body, strong mind, a nice home, beautiful and successful children, righteousness, civilization, refinement, a good man or woman – etc. The Bible says *"You reap what you sow"* Gal. 6:7, so if you put in no work that's exactly what you'll get in return…

NOTHING!

Does that make sense to the person reading this? While going through the Quran, I found that it says the same thing – just in different words. In 53:39-40 it reads *"and that man can have nothing, but what he strives for, and that his striving will soon be seen"*. Now both of these books can't be wrong, Or is it me?

What I came to realize is that..

GOOD THINGS ONLY COME TO THOSE THAT (WORK) FOR IT.

I hope that you can see my angle and agree with me? Now if you can, let me be the first to say that I'm working for this (for us); that I'm working to get my family back, to get my home, ……..but if I haven't put in enough work (don't worry kids) because I plan to give it all that I have and all within my power to live to see the day when you can wake and go to sleep safe, sound and with a smile on your face.

Now if that isn't good enough, I plan to work like a woman does when she is in labor; like there is no tomorrow; just like Harriet Tubman did when she was freeing the slaves!

The formula for "work" is FORCE times DISTANCE, and force is how heavy a thing is, and the speed it travels. Distance is how far it goes. So work is heavy, and moves at a certain speed for a certain amount of time – thus producing the desired outcome. And if you're waiting for something, then you are not in accordance with the formula!

Then I thought about this slogan "TIME IS MONEY", and this sounded so slick rolling off the tongue that I used it for everything. Then one day, I had to face the music that "money would never be equated to time".

I went through all the justifications I could think of, and they all pointed to this one thing: That you make money according to the time you put in. So the question I asked was which one was more valuable, Time or Money? I would have to say that if someone is willing to pay you (a small amount of money to them) for the time you invest for them (which is going to produce millions for them) then your time is much more valuable. If you cannot see that, look at it from an angle that people are willing to pay for your time because they know what it will produce; that no matter how much money you lose, you can always get it back, but when you ever lose time, you can never get it back. That's the difference (a big difference might I add) between the two. That's where the saying "if I could rewind the hands of time" comes into play, but it cannot be done, showing and proving the value of time. So always use it wisely because you will hate to look up one day and wonder "where the hell all the time went!"

What's the value in a name?

If words can heal and words can kill, is there any value in a name, which for all intent and purpose is a word?

Names are giving to describe or represent something – from the characteristics they possess – and when it's in reference to a human the names hold so much more weight. So it is important to choose the names for ourselves and children carefully, because your name gives you a legacy to live out.

Every race of people on the planet has a name that is consistent with their history and ancestors except the black man and woman in North America. Why is that? Well first and foremost they were stripped of their name (while in slavery) and given the name of their particular slave owner, and we still carry this name today, but this was more than just to identify them, it was to keep them from knowing who they truly are and where they came from.

The pages history – especially the Bible – shows that whenever a person has reached a certain plateau in their spiritual growth that another name is bestowed upon them to live through. The most notable are Abram to Abraham, Saul to Paul and Jacob to Israel.

John 1:4 said "the word became flesh and dwelled among men" meaning that it was brought to life through actions and deeds, so to it is the same for the names we are given – be it apart of your essence or contrary to it. So choose wisely …..

If you can for a second, follow my lead …. This mind is like a parachute, and if open it will save you, but if closed it will kill you! So do yourself a favor and open up your mind to this analogy I'm about to give. Now of course this hypothetical and I beg that you entertain it for the sake of this writing.

Imagine taking a puppy from out of the womb of its mother, and not only calling it a cat, but treating it as such. After a while, the dog would be so confused that it too, would believe that it was a cat-basically other than self. Because of the way we treated it, the puppy would eat cat food, try to climb trees, use the litter box, and even try to meow. John spoke in the Bible of this power.

It is conducive to have a name that is consistent with your character and

God, because as the Bible says in Proverbs 18:21 "death and life are in the power of the tongue", so wouldn't it be wise to have a righteous name of God opposed to anything contrary?

That is the questions that all should think about....I know I have!

Natural vs. Normal

According to the Webster Dictionary, natural means – based upon the innate moral feelings or inherent sense of right and wrong held to characterize mankind.

Normal means – according to, constituting, or not deviating from an established norm, rule or principle: conformed to a type, standard or regular pattern.

After reading these definitions and applying them to today is society and myself, I see a lot wrong between the two.

As for me.…..Everything I did was normal, and never natural, but that's because I was easily deceived at a young age that the life I was living was correct. I now know that was a lie. In my neighborhood, struggling with bills, rents, clothes, cars, getting a job, keeping a job, even struggling in school was normal. This is what pushed most of us to eventually start selling drugs! So being in the streets became normal for me –buying, cooking and selling crack cocaine was done so often where I lived, to not see it would alarm anyone – even productive citizens. Along with this lifestyle came drug usage (weed and alcohol). In my family this was socially accepted. I mean my father gave me wine, beer and any other type of alcohol just because. So again I grew up with the idea that it was okay to use. Going to prison even became the norm where I'm from (and now that's where I sit).

Now in no way am I pointing the finger, or trying to judge, anyone with that I'm writing, but instead, my aim is to shed light where it's most dark. It seems that we somehow got these two words mixed up with each other. This has happened because we have unconsciously accepted what the world has said to be right, as the truth, and that has put us in direct controversy with God himself!

If we claim to be followers of Jesus, then we have to apply what he taught and make the same hard decisions he made regardless of how the world feels about it. Contrary to what

we may want to believe, this is not a
popularity contest, and many can bear
witness that Jesus wasn't popular or he
wouldn't have been murdered by the
very government that was set to protect
the land.

Jesus said to "be in the world, but
not of the world" and this is because you
cannot serve two masters at the same
time, so of course, your body will be in
the world, but your mind has to be that
of God! Follow me?

Why is it that everything God says
"don't do", the world says to "do", and we
follow the world instead of God? This
has become the norm and with most of
us, but we don't see it, and since we don't
I'll bring light to some of the situations.
I hope that you can see my point of view.

In the book of Genesis 19:1-38, God set out to destroy a whole city for what was called an abomination in the sight of God. Homosexuality..... He (GOD) told Abraham "that if he could find five (5) righteous people in the city that he would spare the whole town". However, he could not find one righteous person, so the town was destroyed! Even killing the wife of Lot for looking back at the city, after she was told "not to look back" when they were running for refuge. It wasn't only because she looked back but because her looking back was a sign of her not only being in the world, but of the world. Fast forward to today and the world/government/and people in it not only accept the very thing that got a whole city destroyed, but some even participate in this abomination.

In knowing that the first law of
nature is SELF PRESERVATION one of
the best and most satisfying ways to do
this is by abiding to the second law of
nature which is to PRO-CREATE. The
only nature way for this to happen is
with a man and woman, but never with
two of the same sex! Unless again, you
just want to be normal, you can try the
cloning-thing which is definitely un-
natural.

What about the way we use the
words like bitch, hoe, whore, slut, and
chick? We use these words so loosely
when referring to women. I hear this so
much that I have concluded that these
are the only words, (actually misnomers)
to describe a woman -- But what about
words like QUEEN, PRINCESS,
MOTHER, HONEY, LOVE, SWEETY,
BUTTERFLY, WIFE, and STARSHIP. But
again, this has become the norm thanks

to society! So now we have young ladies growing up thinking that it's okay to be called these names so much that they now refer to themselves as such, like it's a rite of passage.

We NEED TO CHOOSE OUR WORDS CAREFULLY WHEN ADDRESSING OUR WOMEN…...I say that because "<u>A NATION CAN RISE NO HIGHER THAN ITS WOMAN</u>", so if that's the case, and it is, the women are our best asset to changing the future for the good! History teaches that for every no good woman there's (a no good man) that made her that way, because she is a reflection of him.

Or just think about the slogan "sex sells" which manipulated the people (men and women) into turning our beautiful young girls into sex symbols. This is not natural-where our women starve themselves (which is unhealthy) to achieve the Hollywood look. They walk around with next to nothing on, revealing everything on their body, that's supposed to be sacred and exclusively for a husband, to the world. And we (men) are no better because we promote it like a savage beast sitting with our tongues out like a thirsty dog. From surgery, liposuction, breast, lip and butt implants are all normal but none of it can change nature, for when father time calls, your body will obey! Getting old is natural – also beautiful because it shows your progress at different stages in your existence. It's like when a tree begins to lose its leaves because of the sudden change in weather. The leaves start to change colors, but these colors aren't ugly. They have their own appeal – even to the person that hates the winter.

It's imperative that we get out of this world (mentally, spiritually and emotionally), but in doing so we will be looked at like we are crazy. Case in point is what Peter said in 1st Pet. Ch. 4...."PREPARE YOURSELF TO THINK IN THE SAME WAY CHRIST DID"...you have spent enough time in the past doing what ungodly people choose to do. You lived a wild life. You longed for evil things. You got drunk. You went to wild parties. You walked in lust. You worshipped statues of God.... UNGODLY PEOPLE THINK THAT IT'S STRANGE WHEN YOU NO LONGER JOIN THEM IN WHAT THEY DO....SO THY SAY BAD THINGS ABOUT YOU.

P.S. Seems like he was talking to us today if you ask me. But who am I except a messenger to the people who want to look, listen, learn and observe.

The Butterfly effect

When an individual is afforded the opportunity to experience transformation from a positive standpoint, it's a beautiful thing, because not only are they changing for the good and betterment of society, but they'll be able to see their faults; mistakes and bad characteristics for what they really are and use them to rebound off of.

Follow my lead......

Just think about the caterpillar- whose essence is a beautiful butterfly – but can't transform into its natural form until undergoing whatever is necessary to transcend. The caterpillar is a wormlike, often hairy insect larva that is considered to be unattractive to almost everyone on the planet. However, the caterpillar has the ability to wrap itself up in a cocoon which is a case usually of silk formed by the insect, and in this cocoon, (protective shield) the change begins.

My caterpillar stage.....

I came into this world with nothing and it got worse and worse as I got older. I couldn't figure out why we had no food; why I had to wear my brother's clothes, (which were too big) to school; why my parents were drug addicts; why x-mas was only a thought in my mind, but never a reality. What was it that I done to this God that everyone prayed to? Did he even exist? And if he did, he had to have a sick twisted idea of what humor was to continue to allow this to happen. These were some of the thoughts that dominated my brain.

It was once said that "all you need to change the future is the mind of a child". This might be the reason why the world is how it is now. Because the people of my age, were cultivated, in the wrong area of things when we were children.

Have you seen him who takes his low desires as God?

When I got old enough to fend for myself, that's exactly what I did! I aimed to get everything I didn't have as a child, (by any means necessary) and I saw nothing wrong with it. While some may say "it's hard to not see your wrongs, or your sins, I differ in opinion because when you're blind, deaf and dumb to the truth…..YOUR JUST THAT! Try to see it from this angle, where the Holy Quran says "that the life of this world is made to seem fair to those that disbelieve". Now, if this script holds any validity then the world (as I've seen it) was fair, (meaning ok). And if the world itself sees what's transpiring as fair then we're all a part of the disbelievers. So when my father gave me alcohol and wine to drink it was okay; it was looked at as cute to see a 4 and 5 year old tipsy. When I began to smoke weed and skip school my popularity heightened. It heightened so much that the girls my age were compelled to have me sexually, which went straight to my head, but before then, they had no desire to be with me what-so-ever.

Everyone my age sold drugs, carried pistols, stole cars, was having sex, used drugs, went to clubs, stayed out all night and so much more. I mean you almost had to be accepted. It became second nature to me. It didn't matter that I was hurting myself, (mentally as well as physically), hurting my family and of course my victims from a direct result of selfishness.

There's nothing new under the sun, and trust me I did it all. I did it so much that I was tired of living it, but what else could I do, (being that this was all I knew) except wish for death? Wishing for it in such a manner that I began planning it, but why wish for death when I had so much to live for? Was it because of my childhood? Because I was on so many drugs, (weed, ecstasy, PCP, alcohol) that I could not cope or function properly? Because I did not accomplish what I set out to do in life? Because I felt like a failure? Because I had no real money? Because I lost the only woman I truly loved? Because I wanted to meet this God that I couldn't see while alive? --Because.....

Well, I can imagine that all these
played a part in my decision to see death
around every corner I turned! I
sometimes tricked myself into believing
that, (I was death itself) and hope and
prayed that I could bring me to some
un-lucky soul. When I actually thought
about it, I had too much pride to take
my own life, but then I figured maybe –
just maybe – I could put myself in a
position to have someone else take my
life for me! No matter how sane I
thought it was, it was the most irrational
thing I ever thought of.

Needless to say, that the plan
didn't work because I'm sitting here
writing this to you, but in a sense it did,
it just wasn't physically. See, I died
inside on 9/13/05, which is the exact date
of my mother's birthday, and when I
almost took another man's life which
ultimately landed me here in prison. I

hoped for the life of me that this man had a gun so that I could go out in a blaze of glory, but he didn't.

The cocoon: While being in prison I couldn't do anything, but face myself (and that was an ugly sight to see). I had to deal with me, and in doing so, I had to turn to where everything originated - - - and that is inside.

The questions that came to mind were: how did I get to this point in my life? What am I going to do now? How will I survive? Why am I still alive? Why did I want to die anyway? Who am I? What about my children? Did I really love them? Am I a coward? Weak? -- And if so, why? My favorite questions were, "how the hell am I going to get out of here?"

As I wrestled with these questions, I slowly began to try and put my life back together, and just like a 1000 piece puzzle, it took time, dedication and discipline. I began to program within the jail, learning what I could, no matter how obsolete the program was. I tried keeping family ties close together, but to no avail. I studied the law as much as possible, so that I would have a fighting chance. Years later, I learned that the studying of the law was almost all for nothing because the Government doesn't follow the law that they make unless it is applicable for them.

I was a long way from where I am now, as I continued to still dibble and dabble in negative things within the prison society: drugs, alcohol, fights and much more. Slowly, but surely the façade I created while living in the streets began to crumble right before my eyes. Not only was I avoiding negativity, but I was also thinking clearer, much more civilized. I was quick to listen and slow to talk. My heart was even softer and I was able to come up with a solution for a problem before the problem ever came about. I learned to be compassionate; I even cried throughout this whole experience which was something unheard of for me.

And thus, a beautiful butterfly emerged, still having faults, but being able to master them on the spot – which was a testament to my hard work. I'm continuously striving for perfection every second of the day (physically and mentally), and being willing to help people when they're in need of it shows my progress in becoming a civilized person. I began to read more to strengthen my knowledge and vocabulary. This is important because it is said (according to the Bible), "that my people are destroyed for a lack of knowledge" and in another place that "the tongue is the most wicked thing in the body", so to conquer these two feats produced a much better man; a person who now opts to think first and then think again before reacting.

When I sit back and think about my "uphill climb", (my transformation) I'm amazed, but not at the journey: the bumps, bruises, the highs and the lows, but instead the reaction I received from my peers. Who, for some reasons, seem like they were very angry about me changing for the positive then continuing to do negative stuff. I couldn't understand it until I read 1st Pet. 4:4, now I can see why I was liked more when I was a savage opposed to now. If that's not an oxymoron, I don't know what is. Then I thought like to hell with them anyway because

I'D RATHER BE HATED FOR DOING WHAT'S RIGHT, THEN LOVED FOR DOING WHAT'S WRONG!

Two sides to a coin

It's a wonder how I can see things now, more precise, than before in the past. That's because back then, I was unconscious; because my heart was in the wrong place. This made me self-centered and blind to the truth, but now I can see with an open eye. Someone said, "That he that increases knowledge increases sorrow; and in much wisdom is much grief." I now understand a lot of what people choose not to.

This is an epistle to every woman on the planet, from me (and may I apologize for all men in general) asking that you please forgive my inconsiderate, un-thoughtful and disrespectful actions towards you. If only I knew the hardships you would face…If only I could fathom the pain you would experience I would remove you from that horrible situation and take your place upon the cross of crucifixion.

"What is it I'm talking about" you ask? I look within my minds eyes at the condition of women as a whole and I'm sadden by what I see. How the men of the world openly mistreat you – so much that you believe its okay. She accepts the names, bitch, hoe, whore, slut, no good, etc., because this is all she hears, (from the very men that are supposed to protect her) about herself. She takes on the role of being a sex symbol with open arms because to her

that is where her beauty lies (so says the
world) and if nothing more than for
impression of the men in the world.

I cringe at how the woman can be
sexually harassed with almost no
repercussions; how she can be raped, or
murdered in some countries just
because she is a woman, as if these
women are the scum of the planet earth,
but in all actuality, they are the Mothers
of Civilization.

I think about the women where
I'm from , who have no support from a
man, or are being used and abused by
one; who can't get a job, but have
children to support, and being that the
man is almost non- existent in their life
they have to depend on the Government
who is cutting funding every day. So
paying rent and bills is just about
parallel to giving childbirth. She tries

her best to escape reality by using drugs
and alcohol, or locking herself in some
church scraping and banging her knees
every hour in hopes that God will save
her. Some even go to drastic measures
by breaking the law to get money for
their family! This is all done to alleviate
the stress, depression and pain that
bombard their everyday life. But to no
avail because all this does is add to it
immensely. How can't I sympathize
when this is exactly what my mother,
grandmother, sisters, aunts and my
children's mother all went through?

The Mother of Civilization

The
woman…Mother…Grandmother…Sister..
.Aunt….Daughter…
Wife….. There is no way possible to live
without her. I mean to be quite frank,
we would all die! Better yet, there would

be no existence what-so –ever. So how is it that we can disrespect and disregard her feelings? Not only that but use and abuse her, (physically, mentally, financially, sexually and verbally)?

In some walks of life the woman is treated so bad that she begins to believe this is natural, and this false impression of reality that she has allow her to accept misnomers (I'm pretty sure that we all can think of a few)as her title. However, this is not natural – it's only NORMAL.

The woman is so sacred and divine that she is used by God himself as the work-shop in which all things will come into existence! What I'm saying is God created woman to manifest himself – so says the Bible with the story of Jesus, and so many other great individuals. Knowing this alone obliges me to not only pay homage to her, but also make known to the world, what seems to be lost? That's the greatness of the woman is our lives! It was once said "that every prayer will be answered through the womb of a woman", in the form of a man or woman, and as I take in the weight of what was said, I have to bear witness to it.

These are some examples of what I'm talking about: The children of Israel prayed and Moses came; the people of Jesus time prayed, and he showed up; the slaves prayed and numerous people showed up – i.e. Nat Turner, Denmark Vessey, Harriet Tubman, and even President Lincoln. When I was younger, I also prayed (because my mother had a drug problem) and children services showed up, took me, my brother and sister, forcing my mother to get her life together (and she did)! This is how

prayers are answered, through the
WOMB OF A WOMAN…...

But please don't be fooled by the
word "PRAYER" because it's only a
disguise for meditation. Trust me.

"A NATION CAN RISE NO
HIGHER THAN IT'S WOMAN" and
they are beautiful queens who should be
held in that regard alone. WE should
never forget that the woman is a
reflection of the man, so if she is in a
bad state of living how much worse is
the man and our nation? This was hard
for me to accept, but I gradually came
around to the truth that when you teach
a man you teach an individual.
However, when you teach a woman, you
teach a nation. She is the first (and
sometimes only) teacher and provider of
the child. Sometimes the woman has to
play mother and father – which truly

show her SUPREME ABILITIES. So I
would like to

"THANK EVERY WOMAN READING THIS, AND EVEN THOSE WHO ARE NOT, and FOR STAYING STRONG AND NOT GIVING UP IN THE FACE OF ADVERSITY.ITS BECAUSE OF YOU THAT I CONTINUE TO STRIVE FOR PERFECTION."

I would just like to reverse the
roles for one second and see if you have
a minuscule of compassion for my pain?
From where I sit, growing up without a
father, not being taught how to be a
man, and watching the struggles of my
mother progress, put me in an
automatic position to rebel against the
world. I became an individual who
disrespected his mother; who fought in
school and eventually stopped going; I

smoked weed and drank alcohol, which led to me selling drugs to support my habit and ultimately taking advantage of my own people's addictions (weaknesses) because of my painful childhood. Knowing my mother was a drug addict made me wish the same pain on every other family, and the only way to accomplish this was to sell drugs to everyone. All this put me where I'm at, at this point in my life. A slave to the white man again! The 13th Amendment pronounced me that, and now here I sit in a cell no bigger than the shower of the person reading this. Everything's been taken from me – not just my freedom, but my money, cars, clothes, women, friends …..Yes! Even my sanity!

Can you imagine living in the same place I just described above with the same – sex (in this case a man) everyday? See, it's not enough that I'm locked down! I have no money, and making less than 18 cents an hour, I have no way to really support myself, so I have to call home for cash to the same people, (women) I abandoned and they truly have nothing! I know this, but sometimes I had to swallow my pride and ask anyway, which hurts me more than any bullet could ever do because I'm taking food from out of my people's mouth. Sometimes, after I assay all the events in my life, I have to pause and take a deep breath. Breathing techniques are keys to my mental stability.

People on the outside always assume that we are okay in here, but this is so far from the truth, as the east is from the west. Being in a place full of murderers, rapists, drug lords, arsonists, robbers – the best of the worst – should convince you that I could be in danger any and every day. Where strength is in numbers, so if you are not clicked up (or in a gang) you become a part of the weak. And anything goes.....

My number one goal is to get home as safe as possible to make amends to my children for not truly loving them the way I was supposed to. See, in my eyes, any person that truly loves their family is not going to do "ONE" thing that will remove him/her from their life. Unless defending their life arises.

With that being said, I had to learn how to see things before they materialized and walk away from situations I wouldn't normally do, but not because I'm scared, but instead because of my understanding. I can't imagine getting killed in jail – that would tarnish my legacy – and killing someone would just solidify my position in prison forever! So I think and avoid crash dummies......

I try to use my family as an outlet, but to write and receive nothing back; to call and no one picks up the phone just adds to the loneliness, and the disappointment of being in jail.

Love

This is a touchy subject for me because of all I've been through which was a direct result of my elementary understanding of the word love. Love might be the most misunderstood word in existence. We learn that love is an emotion meaning that it is a complex, strong subjective response to something or someone.

The vast majority of the world develops (what they believe is love) for someone because of what they can do for them, because of a physical attraction or because of sex. But this isn't love. These are actually emotions that we peg to feelings and call them love, but love has no equal.

Deepak Chopra in *"the way of the wizard"* P. 102 says *"the purest love lies where it is least expected – in un-attachment"*.

We attach so much to the word love, and then when those things change, our love changes too. In the way of the wizard, Mr. Chopra says on P. 103, "when you say you're in love, what you're saying is that an image you carry around inside has been satisfied. This is how attachments begin, with attachments to an image. You may claim to love a woman, but let her betray you with another man and your love will turn to hatred. Why? Because your inner image has been defiled and since it was that image you loved all along, its betrayal makes you enraged ….LOOK BEYOND YOUR EMOTIONS"!

Love can never turn to hate. It is impossible. What you are dealing with is emotions like hate, jealousy, and pain – just to name a few. What I will say is this Love is the mother of emotions. This is why a lot of relationships go through the wringer and end up failing.

Once we realize that love is a universal principle that was used to bring the universe into existence; that love is the essence of all of us. We'll stop searching for it outside of ourselves and go within and only then can we receive love from someone else.

This is how I see love; Love is the highest elevation of understanding coming with a force so strong, that it never can be broken. You can't love someone unless you understand them and understanding comes from knowledge and wisdom, (meaning you must know who you're dealing with by wising your dome to the accumulated information from their ways and actions and this will give you an understanding of the person which will allow you to accept the good with the bad and keep your bond forever.

Once you have understanding, you'll be able to see things for what they really are and not what it appears to be through the third eye-which is the mind!! This will give you the ability to love someone and go through hell, (hell is the imperfections of life) to make it

right!! Now, that's true love which will
bring about peace and happiness. And
that's the real heaven.

CHAPTER THREE
See Things for What They Really
Are
(RESULTS)

Sound/Light
Is There Something Deeper?

As I sit down, and construct this, it is easy for me to see how much I have changed. It all started with a thought, transformed into a word that manifested an action. In today's day and time, we skip right pass the thought (the case of it all) and go straight to our word, transferred through a vehicle called sound, to us. Some of us take this sound which travels at the rate of 1,120 feet per second (without investigating it), on face value.

Someone once told me that a righteous man *"suspects not evil in anyone until thou seeth it. And when thou seeth, he forgets it not."* Therefore, it is easy for some of us to give a person the benefit of the doubt without any proof.

In most cases, this sound is the first element we recognize, but to the discerning mind, sound is but many pieces of a 1000 piece puzzle. That is almost next to nothing. In science, we learn that sound moves slower than light (which travels at the rate of 186,000 miles per second). This light, for all intent and purpose equates to action. The critical of the two is action and the most revealing. A person can say anything and it may sound good; that is exactly what it is, just sound because if it is not aligned with the light that produces the action, then it is just words.

This is why time is so precious and valuable. With it, all things will manifest. You will be able to see things for what they really are and not what it appears to be. Therefore, they coined the phrase "action speaks louder than words," because, what you do in your life, will echo an eternity…will speak volumes about the person you are.

When the light shines on a person's actions, we see with such clarity the truth of the individual, that the words (sound) they spoke only resonate as an afterthought. Therefore, say what you may because the Quran says "*and that his striving will soon be seen.*" (53:40) Never be caught up in the magnetic attraction of a person's words, but only in how they produce, because when it is all said and done, that is what counts.

Armor of God

When I first got this sentence in 2006, my first and only thought was "how I'm going to get out of jail"? My favorite saying was "through the law or over the wall" and I meant that. Then I came up with the craziest idea – that going through the law would be much harder than going over the wall. I know that sounds crazy, and rightfully so, however after seeing how many people get (shafted) when going against "the powers that be" I came to the conclusion that escaping Alcatraz would be much easier.

After a couple of years of being incarcerated, the thoughts died down ever-so-slowly, but no matter how suppressed it was, it always resurfaced in a colossal manner. During those times, I would plot and plan, look for blue prints and different avenues out of the jail. I would build with other people in hopes that they too, had the same urge and would concur with my machinations.

Well, one day in 2010 the urge came back up so strong. I knew it wouldn't be easy, and that I had to start some type of physical training, so that's what I did. I went to my Philly *homie* – a good Muslim dude. His hands and feet were registered meaning that he could be cased up for using them for anything other than self-defense. I wanted to be trained in the quickest way to drop, or even kill) someone if I was ever caught in the act. After explaining my position to him, he silently obliged me. I began working out like there was no tomorrow, to try and get into some type of physical shape. A couple of months later, I was ready (so I thought) and now, I just had to figure out the best way to bring it altogether.

Then one day, I went down to the NOI service (Nation of Islam). There was a brother down there- who was one of the coordinators; a beautiful brother – who was swift and changeable, but always approachable. I decided to bring him to my thought process, just to see how he would add on. He seemed very concerned with what I was saying and actually took time out (by leaving the service) to build with me. He said "I wasn't thinking like God; that in fact I was adopting the thoughts of the devil"! So I asked him, "What God would want to be in prison"? Also saying, "That even the Devil hates confinement." Then I asked him "would it make me any less Godly if I performed (what I considered to be devilish acts) to get out of prison"? This brother fired right back by grabbing the Bible, flipping to a book and telling me to do the knowledge (meaning to study and meditate on it). I looked at this man like he was crazy because I was looking for some insight from him, but he pointed me to the Bible. I kind of felt like he was shooing me away, just to get back to his service. I later learned that just because you don't get the answer you're looking for doesn't mean that the one you got is wrong.

When I got back to my cell that night, I grabbed the Bible and began to search for these scriptures. Ephesians 6:11-17, God's Armor…..

After reading these words of wisdom, I still couldn't make any sense out of them. This was because when I read the book, I just went through it like it was a hood novel. I knew that in order for me to get anything from out of these words, it was imperative for me to study the language, and not only relate it to me and my situation, but also see me in the scriptures for it to apply to me. Knowing that, I had to go back over these verses and see the reality of truth and nothing more.

In every faith-based religion, God is an unseen being that exists everywhere. Knowing that, I asked myself, how I would be able to put on this Armor, unless I put myself in his shoes. Of course I'm not unseen, so let's just say for the sake of this writing that God is a "seen" being that exists everywhere. Now, when doing that I've

seen that the fight I was fighting was
getting me nowhere, because I was
going at the flesh instead of the mind-
set. For me, it was like continuously
knocking down spider webs – thinking I
was accomplishing something, but never
killing the spider, then wondering to
myself why the webs kept reappearing.
The web is equated to my ways and
actions, and the spider is equated to my
clouded judgment, negative thinking
and over all view of things. It was the
root (to be exact) of it all. Being that
you have to save self, before you can
save anybody else, the first act of war
has to be performed on SELF!!! This is
where the principalities, powers, rulers
of the dark world and spiritual
wickedness lie at.

The belt of truth, I would use to
knock falsehoods brains out, and the
same way a belts' used to keep one's

116 | George Hopkins

pants up, is the exact same way I would use the belt of truth to keep me up in a state of Godliness. The breastplate of righteousness would be worn as a badge of honor. Knowing that it would protect my heart from any deceit, contempt, envy, pride, sloth, and greed. The helmet of salvation is nothing more than the shelter that will keep the rain of danger, trouble, evil, and the likes thereof, from penetrating my brain. The sword is the most sacred, and is used when all else fails, also it's an emblem of justice. I'm speaking of none other than the very Word of God. However, these words have to be brought to life by manifesting them in our truth of reality.

After looking back three years ago – and patiently, humbly and meticulously applying the scriptures to my everyday living – I see how I blossomed, how I grew, how I changed.

Now for me to say the thought doesn't
come up every – so – often would be a
lie, but now I strive to destroy all
counter- productive situations instead of
pondering on them. That has made me
a better person. Yeah, the Armor of
God, and if I'm wearing his armor what
does that make me?

Let Go to Move Forward

I was reading something from out
of the *Five-Percenter* newspaper today
that sparked what I am writing now, and
it made me reflect on life as a whole, but
also introspectively. The latter is the
most imperative because self-analysis
and self-examination are the basis for
self-correction. In addition, might I add
that at some point in time in everyone's
life, the betterment of self should be top
priority? Instead of worrying about what
lies ahead, I decided to revisit my past to

precisely calculate what led up to my future (which is now my present) being so grim.

I remember my ever-so-precious mother crumbling right before my eyes due to her addiction to drugs. There were times when my Black Goddess never came home (which would put my brother and me in a position that no child should ever be in, that of survival by sheer instinct). Looking at what I went through up that point in my life (age 5), I made a jejune decision (based off emotions) to sell drugs because I wanted to have money. I never wanted to want for anything again in life; I hated being poor, not having any food, clothes, or x-mas toys. Most of all, I just wanted every child to feel how I felt!

I think it's important to mention that as my mother got her life together, mines was spiraling out of control. That's why, for this reasons and this reason alone, should we be ever-so-mindful of our ways and actions in front of the child who at this tender age – is impressionable and easily impregnated with the seeds (be it good or bad) from their parents/guardians.

To keep the story moving along, let's just say that everything I learned as a child played a major role in my success and/or demise as I got older. Better yet, it was my demise more than anything and success was a long shot.

I sold my first drug (with the help of my brother) at the age of 14, and brought my first gun when I was 15 years young. This is important to mention because at this time, I was still active in school, and a pretty good basketball player who had dreams of going to college one day. This was the turning point for me, or the fork in the road in which I chose to travel the path of least resistance. In no limit of time, I was full-fledged in the streets, and school was an after- thought, if that, except for a fashion show. See, I trick myself into believing that I didn't need to go to school. I mean why should I? I didn't need math because I knew how to count money. I didn't need social studies because I knew the history of the streets (so I thought). And science, why go there when I was a master chemist?

I'm pretty sure that it's needless to say that my mind was molested with these alien thoughts – almost in the same manner as the people of Sodom and Gomorrah 4000 years ago – and I now know this story is relevant to my history. I was once told before that if I looked hard enough, I would be able to

find or see myself in the Bible and
Quran. When I first heard this I
understood none of it and it floated to
the back of my mind the same way the
Titanic floated to the bottom of the sea,
so yes, I can see myself in this story.
Those people had a diseased mind which
manifested in their ways and actions.
And the people of today have a dis-eased
mind, but care not to recognize this, and
I too, fit into this category. No wonder I
struggled with changing my ways and
actions up until the point when I just
decided to let go of the past; meaning to
stop making excuses for the reasons why
my life is in such a debacle. I had a
problem blaming my present life on my
past. For everything I did, I would look
back and say "well this is the way I was
raised", and this thought is what kept me
in the same mind frame as the dumb,
deaf and blind. There's no way possible
to hold on to your past life: people,

places, and things; ideas, perspectives
and/or understandings and expect to
move forward in a positive manner. It
took me a while to learn this, but now
that I have it, I hope it's not too late!

In the story of Sodom and
Gomorrah, God was going to destroy the
city for their thoughts, actions and
deeds, but he gave Lot, his wife and their
children a way out. He made certain to
say, to them (Gen. 19:17) 'TO NOT
LOOK BACK" while you are fleeing
from the city. But Lot's wife did look
back and she died with the rest of the
city- being turned into a pillar of salt.
(Gen. 19:26)

I'm bringing this to your attention
because it is pertinent to my life, but
also to all of us as a whole. Where any
and every time we choose to change our
lives – fleeing as fast as possible from

the destruction that once laid hold of us – we should do so without looking back/or holding on to anything in the past. While this may seem like nothing, it's probably the main reason why we're stuck where we are in life.

At least for me it is. I had to learn to not allow my past to be my excuse for my current situation; but also to never forget it and use the experience as learning tools to push me forward in life; to stop holding to my past. While this was the single hardest thing for me to accomplish – once it was done – my present and future became much clearer.

Peace!

This is a letter that I wrote to a probation officer. Somewhere in our lives we have to learn to take responsibility for our actions (even when we don't want to). Part of taking responsibility for our actions is making an AMENDS. This is hard! To say I was wrong….I apologize……You were right…...It take courage, humility, understanding and respect.

Amends

Dear Mr. Joe,

I'm writing in hope that this missive reaches you in the best of health – not only physically, but mentally, spiritually and of course financially. I also would like to extend my wishes to your family too, but only if you'll allow it.

As for me – if you care to know – I'm doing the best I can, considering the circumstances. I hope, better yet, beg-clamoring as loudly as possible to whomever is listening – Yes, even God, that you accept these written words the same way you would from a person you knew your whole life – and that's with open arms.

Since I've been incarcerated I had the opportunity to recollect on my past life introspectively and so many things re-surfaced that I didn't want to face, however it was an immense necessity that I undergo this painful pressure in hopes that I transform in the same manner that coal does.

I was born in 1981, and my mother and father were drug addicts. I have seen so many things (at such a young age) that would molest the mind of the strongest adult, so you can imagine the psyche of a fertile child. Now, I'm not using this as an excuse for why I turned out the way I did, however, I think it's only right to conjecture that if I was raised under better circumstances that I would have become a productive citizen in society. Unfortunately, it did not happen that way and now here I sit in a place no man wants to be. I am doing everything within my power to become a better person, and in doing so, it is very exigent to make an amends – not only to you, but also to the world as a whole, because when you live as a savage, you care nothing about the people you may hurt in your travels.

Growing up without my father (who was the authority figure in my home and the only man I ever feared) I began to rebel against all men, and especially authority figures. I resented so much as a child; held so much in, and naturally, when we suppress things they will come out aimlessly at different points in the person's life, and this pushes us to do things contrary to our nature.

Mr. Joe, I've made plenty of mistakes in my life, but none worse than the events that transpired on September 13, 2005. I need to apologize for my ILL-ADVISED actions on that day. I hope you can accept this attempt to gain your forgiveness because the sincerity in which I write comes from the most sacred charity. I have learned that responsibility is necessary in every man's walk of life and even though I did not want to embark on that path, I'm glad I did.

It's been many years since that day that almost took you away from your family (and I'm blessed that it did not happen); that ultimately landed me where I am today, but also changed my life for the better. I used to believe that jail couldn't rehabilitate a person, but that was until I searched the pages of history and saw that "MALIK EL SHABAZZ" (Malcolm X) whom was referred to as the devil (while in prison) made a complex 360, turning his living hell (prison sentence) into a University of learning and he came home as a positive asset, instead of a liability to his family. While I have taken many steps in the right direction, I still have a long way to go and I want you to know I will never stop progressing in a positive manner.

Potential

Potential is just that….Potential! It is the ability to be able to manifest your thoughts and actions, but due to a dearth of "Will Power," it lies dormant. Potential……

We all have the potential to do any and everything we put our minds to. This is why it is not hard to see the work of God right before our very eyes, and in some sad cases, we even witness the works of the Devil.

We have the potential to become successful or be failures; to be happy or sad; to be the boss or just a worker; to be positive or negative; to love or hate; to be saviors or murderers; to be strong or weak; to be leaders or just followers, and so many other things that vary between the two.

Some of you may nod your head in agreement, but how many people, truly understand this? I ask that questions because once a person realizes his potential – the skies the limit. The only logical thing to do is to activate their "Will" and kinetically bring it into existence.

It appears to be easier said than done huh? Well, that is the thoughts of a person who has doubt. Doubt will choke the life out of any desire or will. Truth be told, that is what made Jesus such a special and beautiful orator. He was able to transform thoughts into words, and words into actions – which is kinetic energy (at its finest), but before then, it was just potential. I am most certain that everyone reading this has some degree of belief in Jesus, but asks ourselves "how much do we truly understand and believe in Jesus and his words if we are not doing what he said we could do." If he said, "we can do it" what does that make us if nothing more than just like him? Jesus knew the potential that we possess, (which was also in him) so he lead by example and that is the best way of teaching.

No! This is not blasphemy and I stand by that because of what he (Jesus) said. A prime example was after Jesus had spoke and told his disciples of their abilities and potential, a situation arose and Jesus asked the disciples to save a child, deemed a lunatic and sore vex. However, they were unable to do it. So the man was forced to bring his son to Jesus and after he saved he saved the child, his disciples asked why they could not do it and Jesus said

"BECAUSE OF YOUR UNBELIEF; for verily I say unto you, if ye have faith as a grain of mustard seed, you shall say unto this mountain remove hence to yonder place, and it shall remove; and nothing shall be impossible unto you." (Matt 17:20)

Also in John 14:12, he says *"verily, verily, I say unto you, he that believeth on me, the works that I do shall he do also; and greater works than these shall he do."*

He also told us to "<u>seek and ye shall find.</u>" (Matt. 7:7) This is the basis, of the body of work that you have been reading. Seek, is an action word – meaning to do, act or even find. So I say he was saying to…

"TURN OUR POTENTIAL ENERGY INTO KINETIC ENERGY..."

…by finding, (in other words producing) what we are seeking.

Even Paul spoke of this potential by making an immense statement that *"THE SPIRIT OF GOD DWELLETH IN*

YOU." (Cor. 3:16) Now would it not be fair to say that if these words are true, and we act upon them, that we should be able to do (at the very least) what Jesus did? I think that is logical.

The Bible displays so many beautiful things about our potential, and how to manifest it. I personally think that the verse giving in John 14:20 says it best:

"A*t that day ye shall know that I am in my father and you in me, and I in you.*"

I truly believe that Jesus was giving us a road map by saying this. There is no way possible that he is saying this for fun or that "he is in us and we are in him," and we cannot bring forth our potential of greatness just as he did.

CONCLUSION

I would like to thank everyone who reads this for abandoning your comfort zone and becoming a sojourner in my world-, which is uncharted water for you. It has been a while since I started writing these builds and I can honestly say, "That I'm glad I did it." Not because of some type of money, I am trying to make, however, it is the clarity of my life's journey.

I hope, better yet beg, (clamoring loudly as possible) to whoever is listening that someone was able to take something I wrote and apply it to their lives to transform their circumstances into something more positive. Alternatively, even better, maybe

something I wrote would help a person
avoid some of the same infantile
mistakes I have made coming up.

BIOGRAPHY

On time with time is a book of memoirs from George Hopkins; a man that was considered irreconcilable, irredeemable and to some a menace to society. It is the introspective views of a man that made a way when there was no way available. "People fear what they do not understand, and being that change is misunderstood, I shied away from it until I landed amongst the "Walking Dead." For a while, I had no idea who I was, and it took some time to shed this façade for me to see that I did have a choice in the matter. Once I found that out I chose to change; for the betterment of myself and of others."

-George Hopkins

To contact the author, write or email to:

George Hopkins
PO Box 60111
Harrisburg, PA 17106-0111
Email: saheallah@yahoo.com

www.ingramcontent.com/pod-product-compliance
Lightning Source LLC
Chambersburg PA
CBHW061734020426
42331CB00006B/1235